THIS BOOK BELONGS TO:

_____

Dedication

To my granddaughters Elizabeth, Rosalie, and Emelia,
I am voting for you and your future. You are America,
embodying a beautiful heritage of African American,
Caribbean American, Haitian, and Jewish roots. May the results
of the 2024 election ensure and restore the rights that have
been taken away. I have done my part to make sure that
"We Are Not Going Back."

I was born the year of the Selma to Montgomery March, a
pivotal time when African Americans fought to exercise their
constitutional right to vote. Never take for granted your right to
vote. This election is another defining moment in American
history as we vote to protect the Constitution and democracy.
May the day after this election bring the promise of
democracy, freedom, and joy. Be a Joyful Warrior.

With love,
Abuela

'Twas the night before the Election, and all through the land,

The voters were nervous, the stakes were quite grand.

The ballots were sorted by precincts with care,

In hopes that fair results soon would be there.

The candidates prepped with their final campaign,

While pundits and pollsters drove everyone insane.

Kamala in her power suit, breaking the glass,

Gearing up for debates, ready to surpass.

When out on the newsfeed there arose such a clatter,

I scrolled through the headlines to see what's the matter.

Away to my TikTok I flew like a flash,

Refreshing for updates, awaiting the clash.

The trolls and the bots were out in full force,

While fact-checkers worked to keep truth on course.

When what to my wondering eyes did appear,

But a meme of Kamala saying, "Vote without fear!

With a confident stance, so lively and quick,

I knew in a moment, she's here to unstick.

More rapid than fact-checks, her supporters they came,

And she smiled and she rallied and called them by name...

Now Progress! Now Unity! Now Justice for All!

On Reproductive Rights, Climate! Let's answer the call!

To the polls, every city, from east coast to west,

Vote for fairness and freedom, do what's best!

As the debates that before the wild audiences fly,

And the issues that mount as the stakes soar high,

So up to the statehouse, the voters they flew,

With hopes pinned on ballots, and policies too.

And then, in a twinkling, I heard from the news,

The counting was starting, opinions and views.

As I paced in my living room, spinning around,

Election night jitters, to my nerves I was bound.

Dressed in her power, from head to her toe,

Kamala was ready, for whatever would flow.

A bundle of policies she had in her plan,

To govern with wisdom, to lead with a stand.

Her eyes—how they sparkled! Her voice, so clear!

A laugh full of warmth, not a hint of fear!

Her firm stance on justice, her take on the game,

Made me feel hopeful, I was glad she came.

She spoke with passion, she handled with grace,

Her words were so strong, they set the pace.

With poise and courage, she stood tall and proud,

Ready to lead, to energize the crowd.

With a wink and a nod, her campaign set to go,

The choice was clear, and the message did grow.

I felt in my heart, I could rest for the night,

Knowing tomorrow, the future looked bright.

She sprang to the podium, her team gave a cheer,

And away they all rallied, the decision was near.

But I heard her exclaim, as she rallied the night,

"Happy Election to all, let's vote for what's right!"

Thank You for Reading!

We hope you enjoyed *'Twas the Night Before the Election*!
Thank you for joining us on this journey of hope, democracy,
and empowerment. Stay tuned for more exciting stories in the
Coconut Classic Chronicle series, where we'll continue to bring
fresh twists to beloved tales.

If you loved this book, please consider leaving a review. Your
feedback helps us share these stories with more readers like you.

Until next time, keep reading, keep voting, and stay
empowered!

With gratitude,
Carla Henry-Lewis & Elizabeth Lewis

Made in United States
Troutdale, OR
11/09/2024

24535528R00019